planting gardens in graves

planting gardens in graves

r.h. Sin

Andrews McMeel
PUBLISHING®

in fall.

today was much easier

the dry tears beneath my eyes

represent the need to no longer mourn
you

this morning wasn't as hard as the
last

and tonight, i find comfort

beneath the stars

whispering my truth to the moon

using the darkness of the night

as blankets to cover my restless soul

the stars are showing their lights
upon me

and i feel free

i am free from you

alone with you.

loneliness was the reason
i held on to you
and holding on to you
was the loneliest thing
i had ever done

lions.

they threw her into the lion's den
and instead of feeling fearful
she tamed the beasts

the only way.

she was strong
but she was tired
and walking away
became her only option

like home.

in a world

where everyone left me

out in the cold

you felt like home

you felt like love

they fear you.

they're afraid of women

who refuse to sit quietly

when force-fed a bunch of bullshit

they fear strong women

and so they call them bitches

as if their strength is an issue

the appeal.

her sex appeal

went far beyond

the walls of any bedroom

offering.

she deserved the world
and all you ever gave her
was a town filled with misery

nagging.

she wasn't nagging
she was just demanding
you to do more
than you were willing to

just myself.

for so long
my best relationship
was with myself

when people let me down
all i had was me

sacred.

she built a wall in front of her
heart

because she knew her love was sacred

you and your story.

women are living poems

poetry in motion

stories of tragedy and strength

pages of imperfection

the most beautiful stories

you'd ever read

soul first.

fall in love with my soul first

then from there

discover more ways to love me

he's not.

he's not a prize

nor has he ever been a gift

don't let him exaggerate

his importance

to your life

sharp.

women with sharp tongues

cut through weak men

like knives to bread

the friend.

by the time you believe

he's yours

he'll be wrapped between the legs

of the woman

he told you was just a friend

just trust me.

the one they'll cheat with

is the one they'll say

you shouldn't worry about

and they'll always request your trust

while betraying you

in ways you'd never believe

with ease.

you are not difficult to love

your soul mate will love you

with ease

fresh hell.

you were just like my last
you were exactly like the one
before you
you promised me heaven
but you were simply a newer version
of the hell that i've known
many times before

nonsense, your love.

what is there to love
about a person who doesn't love you
how are you in love
with someone who hasn't provided
anything for you to love

better now.

i think i'm better now
i crack smiles and really mean it
i laugh louder than i had before
the thought of you doesn't hurt
i think of you and i smile
losing you was not a loss
you walked away, i dodged a bullet
you left my life and now i'm free

another decoy.

you were just a false representation
of the love that i once thought you
were capable of providing

tales of detachment.

it was never instant
i think when you tell people
it ended
they assume that it was easy

like an axe to wood
it took several swings
to detach myself from you

you broke me down
and so i began the tiring process
of severing our soul ties
in an effort to set my essence free

i walked away

only to return

to your empty promises

of change

asking myself why

unsure of my own strength

telling others

that it was easier said than done

until i finally did it

it was never instant

it was so fucking hard

but damn it, i tell you

it was worth it

the past lingers.

your past loves

still linger on your breath

their dead skin

under your nails

as you once attempted

to scratch your way

to the surface of their hearts

with hopes of finding something

some indication of their feelings for
you

giving yourself to those

who had nothing to provide

but a penetration that never
satisfied you

to completion

keepsakes in boxes and bags
like little museums
displaying the proof
of relationships that fell short
of what you aspired to create

you were trying to fill yourself
with their emptiness
detached from reality
their lies became your religion
and like thieves
they stole from you
then disappeared into the darkness
of every night

leaving you broken
blaming yourself
wondering what you did wrong
as they did nothing right

ease the pain.

all the things

that make you happy

are either harmful

or temporary

and that's what truly hurts

self-medicating the pain

using things or people

that may partially destroy

more of who we are

when it's real.

here's the thing
and i need you to take in
every word

when someone truly loves you
and i'm not talking about
that watered-down shit
that you got from every ex
who caused you nothing
but a great deal of emotional trauma

when someone really loves you
and wants to be a part
of your life

they let go of their past
to better accommodate you
in their future

they don't hold on to past likes,
lusts, or loves
you'll never have to compete

with anyone they've had
history with
because those relations
no longer exist

how or why.

how do you claim
a man who refuses to choose you

why do you continue on
expecting him to love you
when he acts as if he doesn't
like you

please never forget.

they left you

when you needed them the most

you've been hurting

you've been alone

without anyone to lean on

fuck this idea

that you need them

to provide closure

fuck those random texts

and phone calls

that only occur when they

have nothing else to do

but lie to you all over again

they don't love you

nor have they ever truly cared

they don't miss you

that's just the bullshit

they express

in an effort to manipulate

your emotions

you deserve so much more

than what you've had

secured.

here's what you failed to understand

instead of harming her heart

you were supposed to protect it

for the better.

and sometimes a woman

has to walk away

from the one she loves

because she loves herself

too much to settle

for a relationship that causes

her pain

underneath.

i wear my sadness beneath

my smile

but i'm not trying to pretend

to be happy

i'm just trying to remain strong

April 2014.

i'd often feel like

my soul mate

was the hide-and-seek champion

a message to men.

here's the thing
if you're not man enough
to occupy her heart
and love her correctly

don't block her view
of someone better

seconds until.

all those second chances
but everything remained the same

she decided to let him go
because he decided not to change

this was your story.

she thought about the time
she'd invested in a dream
sold to her by someone who made
her fall without any intentions
of catching her

the love she developed for him
made her hopeful
in terms of change
deciding to go back
she dealt with more pain

as insane as it may seem
to you and me
she loved him through it all
yet still wanted
to break free

i don't know.

i guess we get so used

to loving the wrong person

that it becomes increasingly difficult

to be more open

and willing

when the right one

comes along

it was you all along.

that's the thing

i'm almost ashamed to admit

that i've spent a lifetime

searching in others

for a love that could only exist

inside of you

and i know that now

green thumb with love.

if for some reason
i owned a garden
only seeds of you
i'd plant

so with every rose
that grew
i'd end up
always picking you

no judgment here.

even though things changed
you failed to walk away
when you should have

simply because it's always harder
to leave behind
something or someone
who once made you smile
and because of that
it may take you a while

hold on.

if you should ever find someone

who considers an emotional

connection with you

far more important than the physical

hold on to them

know all, say nothing.

i'm way too observant

to be fooled

i notice and discover things

yet i say nothing

because it's entertaining

to watch someone

dance circles around the truth

reminders for men.

just because a woman

is nice to you

doesn't mean she's interested

and just because she rejects you

doesn't give you the right

to call her a bitch

the optimist.

even when things aren't right

in her life

she still finds the strength

to smile

find the words and actions.

it's simple

be more expressive

never let her wonder

or question

her own importance

when it comes to your life

choose her more often

earn it.

you can't complain about the guard

she keeps in front of her heart

while giving her every reason

not to trust you

he'll never understand.

he hurts you

continues to

and you only go back

because he's familiar

you've become so used to having him

in your life and the thought of
anything

different just scares you

you don't want to start over

you've invested so much time

and energy into him as well

as the relationship

but you deserve more

you're way too valuable to be sharing
yourself

with someone who isn't man enough

to understand

the importance of love,

loyalty,

and respect

and yes

i'm talking to you

the dead.

if real love is life

then my generation is dead

vice.

you were my favorite vice

but i had to bury you

with the rest of my bad habits

the manipulation.

your manipulation drained me
i knew you were no longer
deserving of my effort
but i tried until trying
made me weak

the funny thing is
walking away
made me stronger

everything the same.

different faces

same stories

same heartache

same ending

for the broken girls.

there's this negative stigma

attached to anything that is broken

there's this idea that broken things

somehow lose their value

i don't believe that

and neither should you

you're a woman

and though i can't begin to
understand

what that truly means

i can sympathize

as i do my best to remind you

of how powerful you are

never forget about your strength

in times of heartache

remember all the things

you've survived

remember the many moments

when you've played the hero

successfully

saving yourself

this is for you

for the broken but strong

protect solitude.

find your peace
and protect it

you will never
have to compromise
your joy
for someone who truly
cares for you

self-serving love I.

everything you've been searching for
lives within your own heart
all the love you've been longing for
can be given to you, by you

the emptiness of it all.

"i miss you" means nothing without
effort

"i miss you" means nothing without
action

don't let your heart be manipulated

by random texts that read

"i miss you"

and the story goes.

i wanted you

i needed more

you didn't deserve me

the end

you are.

the broken can be beautiful . . .

you are proof of this

self-serving love II.

you are the love

he couldn't give you

not for them.

your soul is golden

but he prefers copper

and that's okay

you're not for everyone

not rejection.

maybe it wasn't rejection

maybe he couldn't keep you

maybe he walked away

so that someone better

could walk in

self-serving love III.

sometimes wanting someone

isn't enough

sometimes you have to choose yourself

not the damsel.

you didn't need saving

you only wanted something real

concealer.

your smile is painted on
but your pain is real

say nothing.

when a woman is tired

silence becomes her language

when a woman is fed up

fighting for what she thought was
love

is no longer

an option

he was.

he blamed your trust issues
but he was the reason

he judged you for being cold
but he was the reason

that process.

people leave too soon
feelings stay too long

begin again.

being single
could be the beginning
of something better
than what you've had

new declarations.

i promised myself
to no longer allow
my physical desires to interfere
with my peace of mind
or the joy in my heart

i see your truth.

your lips, arched with happiness

your eyes scream out pain

competitions.

i walked away
because competing with your past
was no longer appealing

constantly made to feel
as if i wasn't good enough
to be chosen

i no longer have the emotional energy
to keep up this fight

my silence
now a symbol
of my unwillingness
to keep trying

no room.

maybe there's never room

for something new

or something better

because you're always

holding on to

things that no longer

deserve to take up space

how love died.

most relationships

are prison terms

most of what is deemed love

feels more like hell

romance has been

beheaded

and chivalry has long since

been dead

massacred by people

who claim love

but provide something

that resembles hatred

the ending is the same.

she was convinced

that giving herself to him

would make him stay

but he'd always cum

then leave

more than.

perhaps

you left

because i

deserved more

mind in gutters.

soaking wet
a woman creating
rivers of emotion

one year, nine months.

she's the kind of girlfriend

you marry

inherited pain.

children who were abandoned

grow up to love people

who abandon them

what made no sense.

"but he loved me . . ." she said

while touching the bruises

he left on her heart

kept telling myself.

the people who leave
didn't deserve to stay
the people who stay
will be the only ones
i keep

on guard.

but the women

with their guard up

usually love the hardest

fed up entirely.

silence

nothing

she said nothing

she stopped fighting

she got tired

it's over, she's done

the end

say nothing, say all.

a woman's silence

is filled with truth

loss for love.

you've lost so much time

so much of your life

waiting for him

to change

take time.

being single

is a time to heal

i told him.

but when you lose a woman
who is willing to fight for you
you've lost the only thing
that truly matters, her love

questionable restlessness.

what are we

she wondered

lying in bed

holding her phone

waiting for him to call

knowing he wouldn't

the walking dead.

if it's not my ex
it's yours
constantly creeping up
into our lives

trying to maintain a level
of importance
that they don't deserve

i guess
we should bury them
deeper
this time

everything you need.

but you've always been beautiful
you've always had value
don't sex your essence away
to appeal to his image
of who you should be

everything you are
has always been
everything you need

wasting me.

i wasted so much of my energy

on someone who refused

to make an effort

i was always fighting

but no one fought for me

wrong places.

the only reason

you're unhappy

is because you've been

searching for peace

in chaotic souls

i've done this.

we use our unhappiness
as an excuse to invest
our love into people
who ruin our peace

both broken.

what were we

broken and confused

abused by the past

with hopes of a future

that consisted of something real

both tired of a love

that turned out to be tainted

both weary of trusting liars

investing our energy

into the emptiness of loving

the wrong person

we found each other

and lost each other

just the same

hurt people

hurt people

this much was truth

still of value.

single-parent mothers

still valuable

still beautiful

still worthy

still deserving of romance

and love

peace in the morning.

there's a certain type of peace
waking up alone
without the person
you thought you needed
the person who no longer
deserved to lie next to you

at first the loneliness stings
like a hornet protecting its nest
but soon after
there is peace

i hope you get there
and if you've already arrived
i hope you stay there
until you find someone
worthy of you

to serve and protect.

i saw an officer the other day

he stared at me

with the same eyes

of the cops

who gun down

the innocent

and i couldn't help

but pray for protection

from the people

who i once believed

would protect me

to carry on.

my friends are not my friends

my family have become strangers

and the one i care for

has grown distant

i'm alone with no one

in my corner

i'm alone

in search of the strength

to carry on

unreliable friend.

maybe i should've built

our friendship

on something stronger

than binge drinking,

hot clubs, dirty dancing,

and loud music

because when the fun ends

and real life begins

you are never there

you are nowhere to be found

up waiting.

i shouldn't answer
i shouldn't even be awake
between the vibration of my phone
and this overwhelming feeling
of loneliness
i'll let you in
then hate myself after

the unhealthy cycle
of tearing down myself
to a level that best suits
your needs
while ignoring my own

empty and incapable.

real emotions cultivated

by empty promises

and fraudulent love

illusions that i could believe in

illusions of everything

i thought i wanted

i thought you were the one

but it turns out

you were keeping me

from finding the love

that you were incapable

of giving me

no rewards.

there's no reward

for coming in second

in a relationship

that feels more like a race

or competition

i no longer desire

to watch from the sidelines

constantly being treated

as if i'm not enough

always made to feel

as if i am nothing more to you

than a hobby

uneasy after hours.

i should be asleep
overrun by restlessness
this uneasy feeling
of anticipation

i've spent too much
of my time
waiting for you
to show up

we do not.

the woman loves

we call her needy

the woman guards her heart

we call her cold

we

do not

define

the woman

own wounds.

if anything

her scars represent

a woman's ability

to heal her own wounds

what you were.

you were a disaster

hidden beneath wrapping paper

my own personal hell

presented to me as a gift

October's fall.

you nearly broke me in two
the night you admitted
that you were afraid
of being happy with me

your reason.

because the fear

of being abandoned

keeps us unhappy

and alone

first time.

for the first time

in our relationship

i can honestly say

that you've broken my heart

and i don't know how

we're going

to get through this

no confusion.

baby

focus on

your goals

these men

are confused

just no.

no effort

no love

no reason

to stay

best for you.

a woman

who fights

for you

is best

for you

fight for her

unhappiness allowed.

you were lying to me
and i accepted it
because i thought
i deserved to be
unhappy

feeling unknown.

the worst feeling
is not knowing
what you're feeling

people ask if you're okay
and your response is
i don't know

potentially I.

i don't think

it was you

i didn't fall for you

i fell in love

with your potential

to be what i thought

i needed at the time

my search.

the more you're sure about
what you want and deserve
the harder it is to find someone
capable of committing to you
completely

potentially II.

the only reason

i stuck around

was because

i was waiting for you

to become the person

you promised to be

but i got tired

i couldn't wait any longer

organic growth.

my tolerance for bullshit
seems to diminish with age
my circle of friends made smaller
with time

i'm less likely to trust
far less open to what isn't familiar
as even the things i know
appear less appealing

a bit more paranoid
or maybe i'm just wiser
a bit more antisocial
or possibly a little more
selective

life appears differently
the more you live it
maybe i'm seeing more clearly
the older i become

my teachers.

it begins with our parents

those lessons of love

defined by the way they treat others

we watch closely

we take mental notes

that are only apparent to our
subconscious

buried deep within our minds

left to resurface, later on in life

we learn love by watching them
interact

and sometimes we learn about a love

that brings pain and indifference

observing the tension between two
people

who weren't made for each other

i guess that's what happened to me

i saw my father yell and scream

toward the face of my crying mother

i watched him return later with half-dead flowers

and empty promises to treat her better

after demeaning her with words

that i had yet to understand

he'd whisper

i love you

and she'd seemingly forgive him

i'd watch her love this man

who obviously didn't feel the same

but that was my lesson in love

and my teachers were two people

who would later separate

never to discover the truth in what
love

actually is

and sometimes i think that this will
be my fate

living a life

claiming to have loved

when all i've ever known

is hate

years ago.

i chose you
how foolish
my desire to fix you
while destroying myself

my desire to love you
which caused me
to hate myself

i changed the parts of me
you didn't like
i left myself behind
to search for you

and all i could ever find

was more pain

more lies

i fell

you didn't

i fought

i tried

then left

yesterday's ghosts.

haunted by your potential

you'll never be the lover i deserve

hiding.

my anger is a mask
that hides my pain

miscarriage of love.

i was waiting for you
nine months to be exact
you grew just enough
for us to acknowledge
your presence

then one day, you left
without a good-bye
and i never got to meet you

it still hurts me to this day

your palms.

for far too long

i've allowed my heart

to sit in unworthy hands

wake in winter.

i wanted to love you

but my heart grew cold

like flowers trying to push through

the snow during winter

we withered away

4 a.m.

i couldn't sleep

your secrets kept me up

your lies were so loud

your fire.

throw her to the flames
and she'll become like fire

no faithfulness.

sweetheart

stay away from disloyal men

they carry heartache

and disease

2:25 a.m.

we find ourselves

when we let go of those

who make us hate who we are

love hell.

you claim to be in love
but what you've described
is hell

fetishized.

they love pussy
but not the women
they get it from

my angel.

i loved you

but heaven loved you more

i needed you

but heaven needed you more

i lost you but gained an angel

honest lies.

angels

beware of devils

who tell lies

in an honest tone

reentry.

he entered

then left you

an empty shell

don't let him

crawl back inside of you

acceptance.

don't fix her

love her as is

and she'll become more

of who she's supposed to be

shaming.

men beg

for entry

then label women whores

as they exit

men chase pussy

then degrade women

for giving it to them

truthfully.

beautiful souls

torn apart

by beautiful lies

cold nothings.

you gave me chills

i thought it was love

turns out you were just cold

loss.

he bought her virginity

with empty promises and lies

statistic.

it takes two to fuck

and yet so often

only one will raise the child

elastic mind.

i let you stretch my mind
to its limit
testing my mental fortitude
chipping away at my sanity
and i justified the chaos you created
by calling it love

2:58 a.m.

letting you walk away

set me free

all a waste.

so many women waste

their patience

on the promises of men

deposits.

with every thrust

he grew closer

to coming

and once he arrived

he filled you up with hate

this, you and i.

we laugh

we yell

we're happy

we're upset

yesterday we were at odds

but tonight, you are peace

and i am in need of you

why i kept you.

we were both hurt

and so i took you back

because i saw myself

a reflection of my own brokenness

shown within your soul

and i kept you here

because i knew what it meant

to be abandoned

i knew what it meant to be alone

the absence.

you left

but i didn't lose a damn thing

nothing but peace was found

in the absence of you

upon death.

every ex is a death

that brings me closer

to a life with my soul mate

feels.

i feel lonely

when you touch me

the unresolved.

he filled you with disappointment
you hate your father
and yet you only date men
who remind you of him

a reason.

you love men

who don't love you back

because you don't love yourself

lakes to oceans.

i hope you drown

in your own tears

when you cry for me

father wasn't home.

my father didn't raise me

and so i wasn't raised

to be like him

and i'm grateful for that

you used me.

i'm in love with a version of you
that only existed before you got
what you wanted

mothers and few fathers.

women becoming mothers

with men who shouldn't be fathers

the story of my generation

bad or good.

a bad boy

and a good man

are two entirely different things

my own brokenness.

my broken

was attracted

to your broken

maybe that's why

i allowed you to break me

like mother.

your father continued to hurt your mother
apologized, whispered, "i love you . . ."
and she stayed

you are just like your mother

what is worth.

she swore he was worth it

he treated her like she was worthless

my past.

you've seen the stains of my past

and you still want to love me

you've witnessed the weight

of my heart

and yet, you'd still like to hold it

please note.

dear love

your insecurities

are not burdens

lonely people.

lonely people do lonely things
like entertain relationships
that make them feel lonelier

wild but calm.

i believe

that real love

can make the wildest soul

calm down

first heartache.

you know

when i think about it

my father was the first person

to break my heart

underneath it all.

i found myself

covering up the stains

of heartache

with a smile

nightmares begin.

dreams come true

then turn out to be nightmares

a no-good cycle.

avoid making babies

with no-good men

because no-good men

raise no-good men

who will treat other women

the way he treats you

breaking bad habits.

you were the habit

i couldn't break

until i did

it was always easier said

than done

but i did it

instrument.

you are no one's instrument
love, don't let them play you

they.

they always cum
and never finish
you make them cum
and then it's finished
you never cum
they never stay

they always cum
they always leave

without a home.

i realized in the end

that i was at risk

of being homeless

making homes out of humans

his expectations.

he mistreats you
like his father did his mother
and he expects you to stay
like his mother did

love or war.

the wrong love

feels like a war

it changes you forever

a woman's patience.

she has her father's wisdom
and her mother's courage
she has her father's strength
and her mother's patience

she knows that she should leave
but she's too strong to let him go
she knows that she should leave
but she's too patient not to wait

heaven on fingertips.

fingertips

in the roots of her hair

under the moon

is heaven

with your hands

with your fingers

you have the ability

to take her there

lying there.

you closed your heart

and opened your legs

and yet the solitude

you search for

couldn't be found

while lying on your back

one time.

i wish somebody would have told me
that a one-night stand
would lead to one missed call
then one emotional voice mail
letting me know she didn't keep it

better pursuit.

don't feed me lies

then judge me for walking away

to chase the truth

past lives.

all the women you were

in your past

are happy for the woman

you've become

all frauds.

everyone before me

was counterfeit

and everyone after

will be just as fraudulent

no permission.

don't let him dim the light
that lives within your soul

never reciprocated.

i gave you everything
and instead of giving it back
you left me empty

my heaven.

my solitude is peace

my alone is heaven

to myself.

you are alone

in need of more of yourself

touch me.

it's been a long day

and tonight

i'd like to feel nothing

but your fingertips

on my soul

unsafe.

your pussy is not a safe haven
for men who don't care enough
to protect you

the virgins.

nobody told her
that her first time
would make her one of the many
who wasted their firsts on him

all seeing.

she's quiet but she sees everything
she says nothing but she's not blind

this very moment.

right now

your relationship is a nightmare

and even then

you're still someone's dream girl

you may be in a relationship

with a man who hurts you

but somewhere, someone who deserves
you

is ready to appreciate

the woman you've always been

haunting of old.

be careful who you make
your memories with

because doing things
with the wrong people
can haunt you
in ways you never believed

all the time.

they'll do anything
to destroy your peace
then text "i miss you"
the moment they realize
that you're finally happy
without them

your love is not mine.

funny how your love works
but only for you

your kisses only arrive
when you're in need of something

the only time you miss me
is when i've chosen to walk away

maybe you don't care
about losing my love
maybe your only fear
is that you'll lose
whatever i provide

blame.

you changed me

my heart grew harder

my patience dissolved

and the warmth that i felt

escaped me

you made me cold

last night.

i think it happened last night

the last time you'd be able to ruin
me

the last moment in which

i'd allow you to dictate

my emotional reaction

i lost faith in your ability to love
me

i stopped believing in you

i found salvation last night

last night was my freedom

invisible wars.

i fought for this

every minute of every day

losing this invisible war

going to battle by myself

fighting to maintain a relationship

with someone who never deserved

my strength

losing at love.

you care

you fall

you get hurt

you try harder

there's pain

and then there's nothing

you feel numb

sweet lies.

bitter lies

taste sweet

when spoken from the lips

of the person you love

rejected.

silence feels like rejection

maybe that's why this hurts

so much

i stayed.

unworthy and unloved

my only reason for staying

was that change was scary

and the pain you caused

was familiar

safe but dangerous

difficult but easy

you called this love

but this was my own personal hell

and instead of leaving this pit

i decided to stay there

in the silence.

the truth is

i'm drowning

in silence

reaching for the same hand

that left these scars on me

either way.

they make virgins feel embarrassed

for not having sex

they shame women for making the
decision

to share themselves

planting.

i felt so many things at once

my heart's cry was to find

something worth believing in

and the moment i began to let my
guard down

i was faced with a truth

that nearly destroyed my very
existence

i remember falling

this never-ending plummet

into an unexpected

portion of chaos

that would forever change

the direction of my life

i would've done anything for you

in fact i almost did everything for
you

constantly placing myself

in harm's way just to ensure your
safety.

everyone around me could see what i
refused to

hiding behind this notion

that i could potentially love you

i chose to ignore the red flags

that positioned themselves

in clear view but one day the truth

would plant itself in the gardens of
our union

causing us to grow distant

no matter how deep the roots

from seeds of mistrust

and disappointment

grew the strength

that i would later use to walk away

and toward a love that i deserved

never easy.

none of this is easy

each day longer than the last

as i find the hands of my mind

reaching for you

always reaching for you

and at the same time

coming up short

that's the problem with the heart

wanting to be touched by familiar
hands

even if those hands

were the reason for its cracks

what i fear.

patience is the monster
i fear the most
causing us to stay longer
than we should

waiting for a change
that'll never happen

the option.

leaving was the only option
because choosing me first
was never your choice

no passion.

somewhere along the way

someone taught you to associate

anger with passion

and for some reason

the more he screams at you

the more you think he cares

trying.

somewhere along the way
you lost yourself
trying to keep the things
that weren't meant to stay

toward peace.

somewhere along your journey

toward peace

you decided to entertain chaos

confusing it for passion

a type of passion

mistaken for love

a love that only hurt you

in the end

the restless lovers.

3 a.m. is for lovers
and i do hope you discover
a bond that keeps you safe
in the hours of your restlessness

i simply hope that you find someone
to spend those early mornings with
whenever you're unable to find sleep

there's hope.

flawed and broken

i still believe that someone

needs someone like you

your ex.

leave the past in the past

the strongest fires

cannot be cultivated

with old flames

all survived.

the human heart breaks
and continues to beat
heartbreak is death
yet we find ways to survive

we find new beginnings
within the end of everything
we thought would last

we are all survivors
of loving the wrong soul

our sides.

we plant seeds of love

in the gardens of those

who have no intent

to care for us

teach them.

make sure
you tell your daughter
about the madness they cause

be sure to teach your daughter
about the things they do
and say to get what they want

fill her with the knowledge
that your experiences
taught you

September 16th.

what leaves

doesn't deserve to be kept

do you want to.

being unsure

is not consent

being uncertain

is not a yes

emotional pursuit.

you are not yourself
you've become numb,
cold, broken, and fed up
you've been strong
but you are tired
you've been patient
but nothing changed

sometimes it never gets better
sometimes you have to walk away
in order to find peace

don't blame yourself.

women are always doing everything

they're always fighting and not being

fought for

they're always reading articles on
how

to improve for men who refuse to
change

a little piece of me dies when women
write me about the men who hurt them

it hurts me

it's time for men to step up

or lose their women to men like me

i can't imagine my lady dealing with

some of the bullshit i see

on social media, tv, or in the real
world

a woman shouldn't have to provide

an incentive for a man to treat her

the right way

uncaged.

women with wild hearts

are worth it

the midnight battle.

i am strong

but i am restless

i am strong

but i feel broken

abnormal.

i hate the way you pretend

that for some odd reason

the nothingness in your relationship

is normal

i hate that you call that piece of
shit love

remember, never forget.

i'm not doing this to hurt you

i'm just tired of getting hurt

in no way am i quitting on you

i'm just giving myself the opportunity

to be happy

while you made me feel something

i made you feel important

i was afraid to let go until i
realized

that holding on to you

meant holding on to nothing

i was afraid to move on

until i realized that walking away

from you

meant walking toward a better future

losing you wasn't a loss

you, losing me

meant that you lost everything

journeyman.

this much is true

the path toward great love

is filled with disappointment

and our journey is defined

by how quickly

we move forward

away from all the things

that no longer deserve

our attention

yesterday until now.

one day you'll wake up

and it won't hurt as much

things won't improve overnight

but there will come a time

when you'll look back on

what used to make you sad

and you'll laugh

because whatever was meant

to destroy you

will have made you a little bit
stronger

nothing inside.

eyes filled with lies

and the lips that tell them

this hurts because i misplaced

so much of my trust

inside of you

no peace in lust.

let us lie here together

covered in nothing but our truths

until the sun rises

unable to fall asleep

due to the chaos that lives

within us both

restless because of sadness

you and i, broken

incapable of healing each other

dark liquor.

i'm mostly hurt

i drink too much

maybe i'm just trying

to drown my demons

knowing by morning

i'll be on my knees

throwing up my sadness

felt stuck.

i've been hurting

like my wrist cut

feeling broken

but i'm stitched up

overall, i overtrust

then overthink

until i feel stuck

too.

you are not too emotional

being able to feel things

with your heart

is not a handicap

it's not a burden

stay here.

you are beautiful

you are valuable

your life is precious

don't take it

always you fighting.

you're fighting to be chosen
by a man who doesn't deserve
to have you as an option

near death and listen.

so many untold stories

in every cemetery

a garden filled with spirits

who can no longer grow

mouths that can no longer speak

and hearts longing for a chance

to beat again

i hear them . . .

mistakes and tombstones.

congratulations in the subject line

an email from an old friend

ill intentions hidden behind

a message that would appear

to be genuine but it isn't

just the latest attempt

from someone i thought i buried

in the cemetery filled with my
mistakes

devil in the details.

sometimes it's love

or maybe you have a funny way

of describing your hatred for me

hidden behind your smile

is the devil i've chosen

to fall for

reflection of lies.

i should be happy

but i struggle to smile

spreading my lips

to appease others

pretending to be okay

in an attempt to make them
comfortable

i've been lying to myself

when love is hate.

i could pour my entire

heart out to you

and you'll say nothing

you could tell me how much

you love me

and somehow it'll still

feel like hate

after six.

i think it was the silence

and the tension that followed

i swallowed my complaints

and said nothing even though i
noticed

maybe you never loved me

maybe you don't know how

maybe i'm just lonely

using you to fill a void

many women.

Emma isn't perfect

but she deserves the world

Olivia struggles with love

but love lives within her heart

Sophia is broken but valuable

Ava is still trying to find her way

through the darkness that surrounds
her

Mary and Patricia continue to fight

Jennifer and Samantha continue to
survive

Linda, Barbara, Elizabeth, and Maria

will not give in

Susan, Lisa, Margaret, and Dorothy

will not give up

different women, same pain

different names, same devils

stairway to loneliness.

just friends

fuck like a couple

catch feelings

one-sided

fuck a few more times

one-worded text replies

we barely talk anymore

pain, it hurts

rejected and neglected

move on

let go

found someone new

happy with someone new

"i miss you" text

(repeat)

she, a sad melody.

tired

unable to sleep

she sits under the moon

pain swells her soul

while reading these words

with a heavy heart

and a mind filled with questions

she is strong but she feels broken

she keeps fighting but she is tired

she's not perfect but she is trying

she's searching for peace

in the night sky

and tonight, she is you

a heart at war.

it's fucked up but i'll stay

you screw me over but i'll hold on

constantly at war with my own heart

my mind knows the truth

but i find comfort in your lies

i'm alone, even when next to you

as if i'm the only one in this
relationship

alone but taken, alone and taken for
granted

but i'll stay longer than i should

waiting for you to become the person

you promised you'd be

this is my fight, this is my hell

more and more.

you are more than a hobby

you are not his something to do

whenever he's bored

you are more than the rumors

they spill upon the canvas

that is your name

you are more than most men

will be able to comprehend

and that's completely fine

nine years.

most truths

are just pretty lies

weeds in the end.

and here you are
you've reached the ending
you've survived these pages
this generation just like any
other generation before it
exchanging love for hate
investing energy into places
that weaken our hearts
we take our seeds of hope
and bury them deep
in tainted soil
and from those seeds
resentment is grown
pain has become our roots
barely peeking from the ground
trying to reach the skies
but we're stuck
planting gardens in graves

t.

we do not. 107
weeds in the end. 251
what i fear. 211
what is worth. 165
what made no sense. 83
what you were. 109
when it's real. 28
when love is hate. 243
why i kept you. 152
wild but calm. 169
with ease. 18
without a home. 177
wrong places. 95

y.
years ago. 125
yesterday's ghosts. 127
yesterday until now. 231
you and your story. 12
you are. 62
your ex. 218
your fire. 133

your love is not mine. 198

your palms. 130

your reason. 111

you used me. 160

planting gardens in graves

Andrews McMeel Publishing
a division of Andrews McMeel Universal
1130 Walnut Street, Kansas City, Missouri 64106

www.andrewsmcmeel.com

18 19 20 21 22 RR2 10 9 8 7 6 5 4 3

ISBN: 978-1-4494-8717-1

Library of Congress Control Number: 2017950152

Editor: Patty Rice

Art Director, Designer: Diane Marsh

Production Editor: David Shaw

Production Manager: Cliff Koehler

attention: schools and businesses

Andrews McMeel books are available at
quantity discounts with bulk purchase for
educational, business, or sales promotional
use. For information, please e-mail the Andrews
McMeel Publishing Special Sales Department:
specialsales@amuniversal.com.